Estimating the Untapped Capacity of the Private Sector to Deliver Antiretroviral Therapy in Lagos State, Nigeria

CONTENTS

ACKNOWLEDGMENTS

We wish to thank USAID for its support of the research presented in this report. We thank Payal Hathi of Abt Associates for her substantial role in coordinating the field work for this activity, from obtaining Institutional Review Board approval to managing the data collection process and conducting many of the key informant interviews. We also thank our local consultant Adeola Seweje for helping collect the data used to inform our analyses. The report has greatly benefited from suggestions and inputs by Shyami de Silva, Nida Parks, and Ramona Godbole of USAID as well as Caroline Quijada, deputy director of the SHOPS project. Elaine Baruwa of Abt Associates provided a detailed technical review for quality assurance. Adebola Hassan of SHOPS Nigeria and Cathy Thompson and John Osika of Abt Associates also reviewed the report and offered important feedback before its finalization. We thank Oluwaseun Adeleke from the Health Finance and Governance project in Nigeria for his insightful suggestions about policy implications and private provider incentives. Finally, we sincerely appreciate the many contributions of the SHOPS Nigeria team led by Ayodele Iroko for facilitating field work, particularly Modupe Toriola, who provided valuable assistance with logistics for data collection.

1. BACKGROUND

Despite substantial growth in donor funding for HIV treatment since 2002 (Bernstein, 2007) and the rapid scale-up of antiretroviral therapy (ART) to 6 million patients by the end of 2011 (Joint United Nations Programme on HIV/AIDS, 2012), the majority of countries in sub-Saharan Africa have yet to achieve universal ART coverage. In 2009, the World Health Organization revised its ART guidelines to increase the CD4 threshold for ART from 200 CD4 cells/mm^3 to 350 cells/mm^3 (World Health Organization, 2009), which increased the number of people defined as needing ART by 50 percent (Granich et al., 2012).[1] Nigeria revised its national policy accordingly (Federal Ministry of Health, 2010).

National governments and donors have begun to explore the potential contribution of commercial sector health care providers to expanding access to care and treatment, integrating HIV care, building a broader base of clinical expertise in HIV care, and potentially facilitating greater domestically driven HIV care financing. The Strengthening Health Outcomes through the Private Sector (SHOPS) project, funded by the United States Agency for International Development (USAID), selected two countries in sub-Saharan Africa—Kenya and Nigeria—as case studies to stimulate a more informed discussion about the potential role of the private sector in ART provision in this region. Results from the Kenya analysis are available on the SHOPS project website at www.shopsproject.org.[2]

This study of the Nigerian private health sector focused on Lagos State due to a number of factors: the increase in HIV prevalence and need for ART in that state, a high population density with the majority of individuals living in urban areas, a high density of private providers, and relatively minimal security concerns. In addition, the SHOPS project has an office in Lagos State, and the project was already conducting a private provider census in six states in Nigeria, including Lagos State. While Nigeria has tremendous regional diversity, and Lagos State is not representative of the entire country, we believe that the results of this this study may provide lessons learned that can be applied to the rest of Nigeria and to other countries in sub-Saharan Africa.

Lagos State, Nigeria

Lagos State is the commercial heart of Nigeria. It comprises five administrative divisions: Badagry, Epe, Ikeja, Ikorodu, and Lagos. Over 85 percent of the state's population resides in metropolitan Lagos, an area covering 37 percent of the land area of Lagos State. With over 20,000 persons per square kilometer in some areas, Lagos State has the most densely concentrated population in Nigeria (Lagos State government).

The HIV epidemic in Lagos is somewhat more severe than in Nigeria as a whole, with a prevalence of 5.1 percent compared to national estimates of 4.1 percent, although there are thirteen states in the country with higher HIV prevalence (Nigerian National Agency for the Control of AIDS, 2012).

---

[1] CD4 cells (sometimes called T-cells) are a type of lymphocyte (white blood cell)—an important part of the immune system.

[2] Banke, K., J. Ugaz, S. Resch, J. Jackson, M. Chatterji, A. Talib, and E. Sanders. 2014. *Estimating the Untapped Capacity of the Private Sector to Deliver Antiretroviral Therapy in Kenya.* Bethesda, MD: Strengthening Health Outcomes through the Private Sector Project, Abt Associates.

Targets in the National HIV/AIDS Strategic Framework for 2010 to 2015 call for at least 80 percent ART coverage of adults in need of treatment by 2015; the national baseline value was 32 percent. Current data on unmet need for ART among adults in Lagos State are lacking, but recent records of public facilities providing ART published by the Ministry of Health of Lagos State show that, as of September 2012, 47,920 adults (aged 15 and above) with advanced HIV infection had been started on ART at some point, and 38,084 of them were receiving ART.[3]

In Nigeria, commercial providers have proliferated since the mid-1980s, and faith-based and commercial providers are estimated to provide 80 percent of health services nationally (Kombe et al., 2009). The private sector serves Nigerians from all socioeconomic classes. Data show that 64 percent of Nigerians in the lowest wealth quintile and 51 percent in the highest wealth quintile receive care from commercial providers (International Finance Corporation, 2007).

ART in Lagos State is provided primarily through public hospitals, where patients can receive comprehensive HIV services, including free antiretroviral medications. Public sector ART facilities often have high patient loads and insufficient staff, and patients face long waiting times (Health Reform Foundation of Nigeria, 2007). A recent census of private providers showed that there are a total of 1,736 private facilities (clinics, health centers, hospitals, and nursing or maternity homes) in Lagos State (Johnson et al., 2014). Of these, 65 percent offered HIV testing and counseling, but just 10 percent self-identified as ART providers for adults. The private sector ART providers were concentrated in the divisions of Ikeja (101 providers) and Lagos (49 providers).[4] However, the ART patient volume among private providers was low, varying from nearly three patients per facility receiving ART at nursing homes, to four patients per facility for clinics, and up to 11 and 12 for hospitals and medical centers, respectively. Only two private providers in the state saw more than 100 ART patients. In contrast, a recent survey of 23 public ART providers in Lagos State showed that all of them had over 100 patients, and 10 out of 17 who reported patient volume each saw over 900 patients (Katz et al., 2012).

Lagos State has a large number of health care providers, with an estimated 41 physicians per 100,000 population, compared to the national average of 21 physicians per 100,000 population (Federal Republic of Nigeria, 2007). The large number of providers presents an opportunity for innovative engagement of the private commercial health sector. Many commercial providers provide some HIV-related services, and some provide ART, but usually to a small volume of patients. There has been no significant formal effort by the Nigeria Federal Ministry of Health or the Lagos State Health Commission to encourage and support private sector provision of ART.

This study aims to explore commercial providers' interest in ART provision, identify perceived barriers in expanding commercial sector provision of

[3] Six facilities did not report data. The actual number of individuals receiving ART may be as high as 53,000, if these six facilities have patient volumes equal to the average of the 17 facilities reporting.

[4] Lagos State comprises 20 local government areas that are grouped into five administrative divisions.

ART, and quantify the potential impact on ART coverage (based on providers' responses about their willingness to provide ART and their slack capacity to increase the number of patients treated). Increased commercial sector provision of ART could potentially reduce unmet need[5] and ease the burden on the public sector, while providing ART services to those who may be able to pay for them. It could also enable patients to receive care closer to home. In addition, wealthier patients being served by the public sector may be able to shift to the commercial sector, allowing the public sector to serve additional patients who are not receiving treatment.

To our knowledge, no systematic effort has been made to estimate the potential impact of a greater engagement of the private commercial sector in ART service delivery in Nigeria. This study uses data from multiple sources for an analysis that aims to stimulate discussion about the potential expansion of ART service delivery through the private commercial sector in Lagos State. We explored two questions:

1. What is the estimated untapped capacity of commercial providers to scale up ART provision?

2. What barriers hinder the ability of commercial health providers to start or expand ART provision?

For the purposes of this report, "capacity" refers to resources needed for the delivery of HIV services, including the number of employees, available staff time, staff skills, and equipment. "Private"—as in "private sector" or "private providers"—refers to "commercial."

The next section presents the methods used to estimate the capacity of the commercial sector to increase the number of adults with HIV who receive ART. Given the complexity and specificities of pediatric HIV care, the study scope was limited to adult HIV treatment. Section 3 highlights the findings from surveys of private facilities and includes estimates of the potential additional commercial sector capacity to deliver ART services. Section 4 discusses the implications of the findings and their relevance for policymakers.

5 For the purposes of this study, unmet need is defined as the number of people living with HIV who are eligible for ART services but are not receiving them.

Partnership for Transforming Health Systems Phase II

2.   METHODS

As seen in the following figure, the maximum plausible amount of private sector capacity that could be made available for ART scale-up is limited by the number of private providers who have the capacity to scale up ART (for instance, certain groups of private providers, such as radiologists, would not be expected to play a role in ART provision) and those who are interested in either starting or scaling up ART provision. The potential impact may be further constrained by the location of providers relative to the HIV-positive population distribution within a country, and by the abundance or lack of options for ART in the areas where they live. Further, potential providers may have variable levels of readiness. Some may be trained and equipped to deliver ART, while others may have the potential but require some additional investment in the form of ART-specific training, information systems, laboratory access or capacity, or other technical needs essential for delivering high quality ART services. Of these providers, a portion of their work day is already spent delivering non-ART care to private patients (and possibly to patients in the public sector as well, among providers who practice in both sectors). Therefore, the potential amount of private sector effort available for ART among existing providers who are interested in starting or scaling up ART provision can come from three sources: (1) increases in hours worked; (2) increases in productivity, which includes decreasing downtime and increasing relative output; or (3) substitution of non-ART service provision for ART service provision.

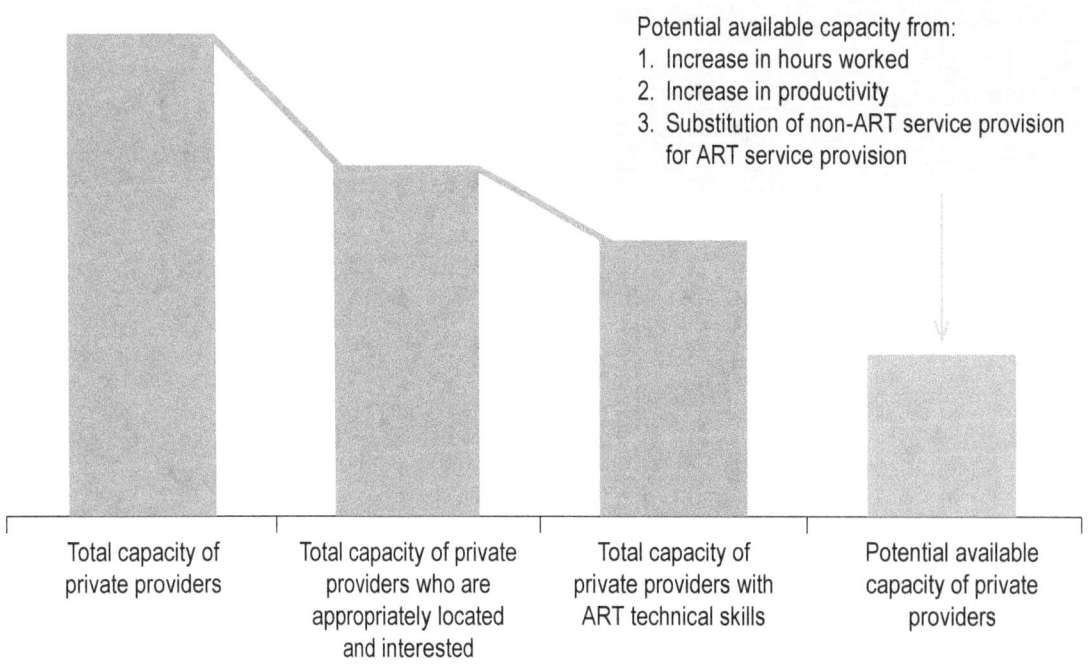

Potential of the Private Sector to Provide Antiretroviral Therapy

Potential available capacity from:
1. Increase in hours worked
2. Increase in productivity
3. Substitution of non-ART service provision for ART service provision

| Total capacity of private providers | Total capacity of private providers who are appropriately located and interested | Total capacity of private providers with ART technical skills | Potential available capacity of private providers |

This report uses the term "slack capacity" to describe the resources (human or physical) and time not being used that could be employed to provide ART to additional patients without adding any extra resources. This concept is important because it helps donors, policymakers, and program implementers understand how much flexibility any facility has to increase the number of patients it can treat relative to the facility's patient volume.

We conducted a mixed-methods analysis with four components: a literature review and data analysis, a survey of facility managers, interviews with stakeholders, and estimation equations. We conducted a thorough literature review of existing reports and policy documents related to ART in Nigeria and reviewed relevant national data sets to identify information that could be incorporated into the analysis.

In November and December 2012, we surveyed a sample of 40 managers of private facilities (including 14 that were providing ART at the time of the study). We collected information on their HIV service provision, interest in providing ART, capacity to provide it, and perceived barriers to its provision. A variety of facility types were selected across the five divisions of Lagos State. Table 1 shows the distribution of surveyed facilities by division and facility type. Ikeja and Lagos divisions are part of metropolitan Lagos, while Badagry, Epe, and Ikorodu are not part of metropolitan Lagos. We surveyed more facilities in those divisions with higher HIV prevalence. We asked managers for information at the facility level on staffing, services provided, patient volume, perceived barriers to ART provision, the capacity of their facilities to deliver ART services, and their interest in providing the treatment.

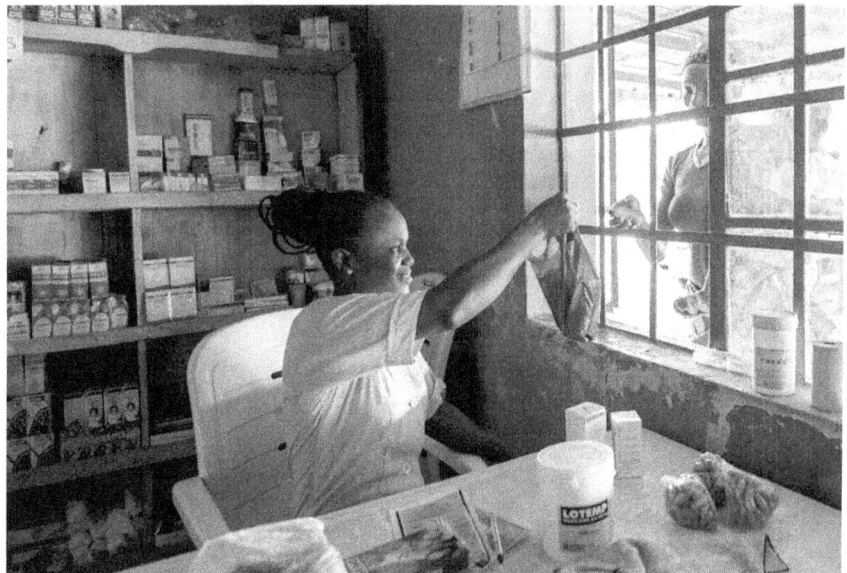

Partnership for Transforming Health Systems Phase II

Table 1. Survey Sample Summary

Division	Adult HIV prevalence*	Population (in millions)	Universe of private providers **	Number of facilities surveyed			
				Clinics	Health centers	Hospitals	Total
Badagry	5.4%	1.8	297	4	2	4	10
Epe	4.6%	0.3	16	2	0	1	3
Ikeja	5.0%	4.8	903	2	0	6	8
Ikorodu	5.1%	0.5	107	0	0	3	3
Lagos	5.3%	1.5	362	4	0	12	16
Total	5.1%	9.0	1,685	12	2	26	40

*Source: Nigerian National Agency for the Control of AIDS, 2012.

**Source: SHOPS Nigeria Private Health Facility Census (Johnson et al., 2014).

Note: Numbers may not add due to rounding.

We conducted open-ended interviews with 13 representatives of key stakeholder groups[6] about their perceptions of ART quality in the private sector, referral mechanisms, provider business models (including payment and reimbursement mechanisms), and barriers to the expansion of ART provision.

We developed a series of equations to estimate the plausible number of additional ART cases that could be served by increasing the involvement of the private sector. We used information from the interviews and the survey of private facilities, along with publicly available secondary data. The equations, variables, and assumptions are included in the annex. We relied on the primary data collected for this study to inform assumptions about the likelihood of participation, ART service volume, and barriers to implementation.

[6] Five informants were from the public sector (the Ministry of Health, the Nigerian Institute of Medical Research, and the Lagos State AIDS Control Agency). The remaining eight were from the private sector, including the Institute of Human Virology, the AIDS Prevention Institute, medical associations, one laboratory, business coalitions, and nonprofit networks and foundations.

3. FINDINGS

The surveys of private facility managers and interviews with key informants revealed that inadequate provider expertise, insufficient laboratory resources, and other barriers impede greater ART provision at many private health facilities. However, our estimates suggest that the commercial sector has ample capacity to scale up ART services and reach the estimated 53,620 people with unmet need for ART in Lagos State. This section discusses findings from the private provider survey and key informant interviews, as well as our estimates of potential private provider capacity to deliver ART.

Sample Overview

We interviewed 40 managers of private facilities. A total of 310 medical doctors worked at these facilities in a full- or part-time capacity. Roughly 13 percent of the medical doctors also worked at least part-time in the public sector. Table 2 summarizes the main characteristics of the facilities included in our survey. ART was provided at 35 percent of the facilities, which included 12 clinics, 2 health centers, and 26 hospitals.

Table 2. Characteristics of Sample Facilities, by ART Status

	ART providers	Non-providers of ART	All providers
Number of facilities	14	26	40
Total FTE employees	232	427	659
FTE clinicians	91	142.5	233.5
General FTE medical staff	141	284.5	425.5
Average FTE employees by facility type	17.9	16.4	16.9
Clinics	6.9	5.07	5.7
Health centers	0	2.25	2.3
Hospitals*	22.7	22.8	22.8
Percent of clinicians who also work in public sector**	27.7	4.2	13.2
Average annual outpatient volume	4,109	17,651	13,137
Average ratio of annual outpatients per FTE clinician	480.8	4,863.6	3,402.7

Note: FTE = full-time equivalent

* One facility (Lagoon Hospital) was missing data on several variables, including number of employees.

**It was not possible to know whether clinicians working in the public sector were working there in a full- or part-time capacity. Therefore, the percentage of clinicians also working in the public sector is expressed as a fraction of the total number of clinicians, not FTE employees.

The number of full-time equivalent (FTE) medical doctors, specialists, resident nurses, and other health care workers was estimated by counting any employee reported as full-time as one FTE employee, and by counting any part-time employee as one-half of an FTE employee. There were a total of 659 FTE employees in the surveyed facilities, with 233.5 of these FTE employees representing clinicians (i.e., medical doctors and specialists) and 425.5 representing general medical staff (resident nurses and other health care workers). The average number of FTE employees was similar for facilities providing ART (17.9) and for those not providing ART (16.4). Facilities not providing ART had a much higher annual average patient volume than those providing ART. Thirteen of the 17 hospitals not providing ART reported outpatient volumes of over 10,000 per year, while just two of the hospitals providing ART reported outpatient volumes in that range.

Potential Capacity of the Private Sector to Provide ART

We used data from the private facility survey and secondary data sources to estimate the potential number of additional people living with HIV (PLHIV) who could receive ART if the private sector's slack capacity were fully used. These estimates were done at the division levels. Table 3 summarizes key inputs into the equations. (See the annex for a detailed description.)

In the facility survey, managers were asked to provide information on how many more patients they could treat each day. Most managers (93 percent) stated that they could treat more patients on a daily basis. Private facilities could serve a relatively high number of patients for any type of visit (not just ART): 48.5 percent said their facilities could treat an extra one to 10 patients per day, 21.5 percent said an extra 11 to 20 patients would be possible, and 30 percent said they could treat more than 20 extra patients per day.

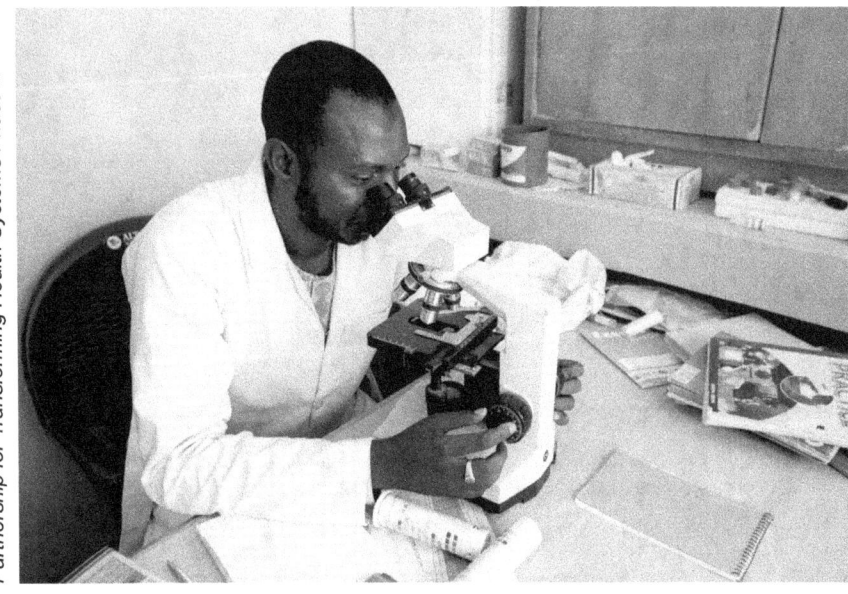

Partnership for Transforming Health Systems Phase II

Table 3. Potential Additional ART Contribution from Private Facilities

Division	Total private health facilities*	Private facilities sampled	Sampled facilities willing to expand or start ART service	Potential additional outpatient visits per workday among sampled facilities willing to expand or start ART service	Potential additional ART cases per year among sampled facilities willing to expand or start ART service
Badagry	297	10	1	130	433
Epe	16	3	1	16	178
Ikeja	903	8	4	159	1,176
Ikorodu	107	3	2	34	378
Lagos	362	16	7	231	987
Total	**1,685**	**40**	**15**	**570****	**3,152****

*The number of private health facilities was obtained from the SHOPS private health facility census (Johnson et al., 2014). All other figures in the table were obtained from our private facility survey.

**These numbers represent overall totals for Lagos State. However, our estimations relied on numbers at the division level separately for providers delivering ART or not delivering ART.

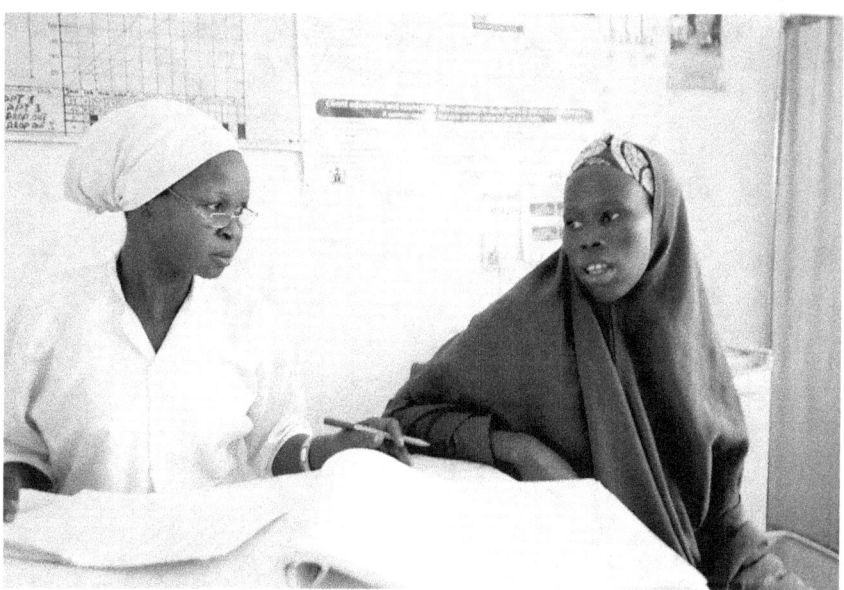

Partnership for Transforming Health Systems Phase II

7 The number of clinicians interested in delivering ART was calculated by multiplying the number of FTE clinicians by the percentage of doctors the manager of each facility said would be interested. The question did not ask for an exact percentage but rather the following categorical ranges: none, < 10%, 10–29%, 30–49%, 50–69%, 70–89%, > 90%, and all. With the exception of the first and last categories, we chose the middle points of each option (5%, 19.5%, 39.5%, 59.5%, 79.5%, and 95%) and coded the first and last categories as 0% and 100%, respectively.

10 In terms of increased workload, assuming that an average of 186 additional ART patients each requires six visits per year equates to a total of approximately 1,100 additional visits annually. Assuming that a doctor can see 20 patients a day for 200 days per year, or a total of 4,000 patient visits per year, then an additional 1,100 visits represents approximately 28 percent of a full FTE's workload. These data suggest that the providers surveyed are currently working at approximately 72 percent capacity.

Clinician interest in providing ART varied by the ART provision status of each facility. (A facility that provides ART may include clinicians who provide ART and those who do not.) In the 26 facilities not providing ART, 67 percent of the clinicians were interested in providing the treatment. In contrast, among the 14 facilities providing ART, willingness (among providers in those facilities not providing ART) was considerably lower, at just 35 percent.[7] The most common reasons for lack of interest in providing ART were cost, lack of training or skills, and concerns about increased workload. We estimated how many additional patients each of those facilities that provide ART could treat. Assuming that each patient pays an average of six ART-related visits to the facility per year,[8] we divided the number of extra patients that facility managers reported they could see (without an increase in hours worked) by the number of FTE clinicians.[9] Based on this calculation, we estimated that facilities, regardless of ART provision status, could take an average of 186 additional ART patients per year for each FTE clinician.[10] The results showed that facilities not providing ART could treat a larger number of new ART patients (237 per FTE clinician) than facilities providing ART (89 per FTE clinician).

When we asked the managers of all 26 facilities that were not providing ART as to whether they would be interested in providing the treatment, only one facility indicated that none of their providers were interested. All facility managers were asked why they thought some medical doctors in their facilities would not be interested in providing ART. The most common answers were "lack of training or skills" (32 percent), "concerns that ART would increase their workload too much" (15 percent), "costs" (12 percent), and "lack of resources or capacity" (12 percent).

We used this information and the data in Table 3 to calculate the number of additional PLHIV who could receive ART services through the private sector in Lagos State if slack capacity were used. The capacity for each division in Lagos State is presented in Table 4, along with our estimate of unmet need for ART in each division. The equations used to produce these estimates are presented in the annex.

Table 4. Estimated Private Sector Capacity to Deliver ART and Fill Unmet Need

Division	A. Estimated unmet need (in number of ART patients)	B. Estimated capacity of private sector	C. Potential number of additional ART cases treated (minimum of A and B)	D. Estimated proportion of unmet need that could be filled by private sector
Badagry	9,250	51,506	9,250	100%
Epe	2,737	1,120	1,120	41%
Ikeja	36,725	307,126	36,725	100%
Ikorodu	4,907	15,708	4,907	100%
Lagos	0*	75,781	0	N/A
Total	53,620	451,241	52,002	97%**

Notes: Numbers may not add up due to rounding. Estimates were obtained using the set of equations displayed in the annex. The specific calculations are available from the authors upon request.

*According to our estimates, there were no people in Lagos division who were eligible for ART services but not receiving ART.

**This percentage is the total of column C divided by the total of column A.

Our findings suggest that under optimal conditions, private facilities in Lagos State could treat approximately 52,000 additional persons requiring ART and therefore potentially fill all of the current unmet need in most divisions and 97 percent of overall unmet need in Lagos State. Our estimates show that private providers could take on about 451,000 additional ART cases, which far exceeds the estimated 53,620 individuals who are eligible for but not receiving ART. However, at the division level, the distribution of unmet need and slack capacity at facilities varies. In two of the five divisions (Badagry and Ikorodu), a modest scale-up could more than meet any need not currently served. The private sector is especially capable of adding patients in Ikeja division, with providers able to take more than eight times the current unmet need. However, in Epe division the number of people who are eligible for ART but are not receiving it still exceeds the number of cases that could be served by the existing private providers.

In our estimations, we observed that the amount of ART delivered in Lagos division (particularly Lagos mainland district) far exceeded the estimated prevalence of treatment-eligible HIV cases originating in that division, which caused our estimated unmet need in Lagos division to be zero. It is possible that our estimation of HIV prevalence is too imprecise to pick up a highly concentrated, hyper-local epidemic, and that need for ART is higher in Lagos division than we estimated. However, a more plausible explanation is that a substantial number of PLHIV from other divisions in Lagos State travel to Lagos division to seek ART services. We were not able to determine the origin of patients receiving ART in Lagos division, and therefore we could not determine whether there is still unmet need among PLHIV living in this division despite the sufficient quantity of treatment slots in Lagos division ART sites.

It is clear that there is unmet need that could be mitigated by expanding private sector ART provision at the state level. More work is needed to understand treatment-seeking behaviors as well as the home origin of ART clients at treatment sites.

Even under conservative assumptions about the proportion of private facilities that are willing to start or expand ART delivery, potential reductions in unmet need could still be substantial. For example, even if just 10 percent of facilities were willing to expand or start ART delivery and barriers to doing so were addressed, unmet need for ART in Lagos State could be reduced by 95 percent (see Table 5).

Table 5. Potential ART Cases and Reduction in Unmet Need for ART

Division	Unmet need (number of ART patients)	Proportion of unmet need that could be reduced if the following percentage of private facilities were willing to expand or start ART service:		
		10%	20%	37.5%
Badagry	9,250	100%	100%	100%
Epe	2,737	10%	19%	41%
Ikeja	36,725	100%	100%	100%
Ikorodu	4,907	100%	100%	100%
Lagos	0	N/A	N/A	N/A
Total	53,620			
% Reduction in unmet need		95%	96%	97%

Notes: The private facility survey results showed that 37.5 percent of facilities were willing to expand or start ART service, so this level was used as the upper bound for this analysis. Numbers may not add up due to rounding.

Barriers

Several barriers must be addressed to tap the potential capacity for ART in the private sector. In the provider survey, providers were asked several questions regarding barriers to expanding ART provision. When asked to name the most important barrier for ART providers, facility managers most commonly cited three barriers: laboratory capacity (31 percent of ART providers and 36 percent of non-providers), financing the cost of treatment (46 percent of ART providers and 8 percent of non-providers), and provider expertise (8 percent of ART providers and 28 percent of non-providers) (see Table 6). No providers reported that inadequate provider time would be a barrier. All of the facility managers reported that they usually refer HIV patients to the public sector for ART-related services they do not have; 38 percent of these referrals are for outpatient treatment and 26 percent are for inpatient treatment.

Table 6. Most Important Barriers to ART Provision Reported by Private Facility Managers (%)

Barrier	ART providers (n = 13)	Non-providers of ART (n = 25)	All providers (n = 38*)
Laboratory capacity	31	36	34
Financing the cost of treatment	46	8	21
Provider expertise	8	28	21
Need to improve record-keeping systems	0	16	11
Need to add pharmacy services	8	8	8
Need additional clinic space	8	4	5

Note: The number of providers is less than 40 because two were missing data on the most important barriers to ART provision.

Several of the 13 key informants interviewed highlighted inadequate infrastructure, provider expertise, and concerns about ensuring quality of services as important barriers to scaling up ART services in the private sector. In terms of infrastructure, many noted that private facilities are often small and have few employees with high staff turnover. Several raised concerns about whether smaller private facilities would have adequate staffing to manage ART, and noted that because of high staff turnover, they need to constantly train new staff. Several mentioned the need to offer training and ongoing mentoring that fits into the schedules of private providers and minimizes time away from their businesses. Others noted that easier access to government trainings would be beneficial for private providers, particularly if they do not have to pay.

Some private facilities have laboratories, but as these are expensive to maintain, some key informants suggested further developing a "cluster" model. In this model, a government facility would handle diagnosis and testing services for a group of public and private facilities. Patients could access ART through private facilities within the cluster. Others mentioned that an improved system of accreditation, monitoring, and auditing should be implemented for laboratories.

The main barriers to scale-up were laboratory capacity, financing treatment, and provider expertise; also inadequate infrastructure and concerns about ensuring quality.

Many key informants felt that the current quality and capacity of private providers is variable. They tend to be concentrated in areas that are already served by primary health centers or public hospitals, so informants felt their added value in being able to reach the underserved is unclear.

Stigma was an additional barrier reported by several key informants. People may be afraid to go to facilities known for treating people with HIV and AIDS, and private providers may fear losing business if they become known as HIV and AIDS treatment facilities. However, patients may prefer private sector facilities because of greater anonymity and privacy, and informants noted that some people living with HIV are willing to pay for health care in the private sector simply because of its perceived privacy. An HIV and AIDS anti-discrimination bill passed in April 2014 aims to prevent HIV-related discrimination and stigmatization. This legislation may encourage more voluntary testing and counseling as well as access to ART, while reducing the fears of some private providers about losing business.

Many informants raised financial issues as barriers to further engaging the private sector in ART provision. ART is excluded from the national health insurance scheme, but there has been some recent discussion about including antiretroviral drugs. ART is covered by some private health insurance plans, but few Nigerians are covered by private insurance. ART is provided for free in the public sector, and Lagos State mandates that HIV care should be provided free of charge to those in need. Since most private hospitals or clinics are commercial, many key informants raised concerns about how to enable private facilities to provide free ART services, or how to reimburse them for services so that they both cover costs and make a reasonable profit. Otherwise, the incentives are unclear for private facility participation.

Finally, informants noted that there is no effective framework in place for how the public sector can partner with the private sector at the national or state levels. The National Policy on Public Private Partnership for Health has existed since 2005, but has not been developed into a concrete implementation framework. Though national and state level strategic plans mention engaging the commercial sector in ART expansion, this has not been achieved due to insufficient coordination between the public and private sectors and the lack of a clear public-private partnership agreement or policy.[11] Building and strengthening the capacity of public-private partnership units at the state and federal levels is necessary to create an enabling policy environment for the private health sector.

Opportunities

The private sector is a major source of health care in Nigeria that already provides certain HIV services, according to informants. Public and private sector informants generally agreed that working with the private sector to deliver ART would be feasible and desirable to meet the country's unmet ART need.

Many factors in the current national policy framework could be leveraged to facilitate more extensive engagement with the private sector to scale up ART provision. The national HIV/AIDS strategic framework from 2010 to 2015 noted that a multisectoral partnership that includes the private sector would be a cornerstone of the national HIV response (Nigerian National Agency for the Control of AIDS, 2009). Without providing details on how the private sector would become involved, the 2010 national ART guidelines recognize that "the private sector is a dominant stakeholder" and that "private sector collaboration is essential because patients access care in both private and public facilities" (Federal Ministry of Health, 2010). ART is mentioned in the list of services that the private sector can provide, as long as a facility meets the following criteria:

- Registers service with the appropriate government agency.
- Adopts a unified monitoring and evaluation plan, including the use of standardized tools for data collection. Data must be reported to the national monitoring and evaluation unit, as requested by the coordinating body.
- Promotes and displays government regulations on fee exemptions relevant to HIV and AIDS.
- Is open to regular inspection and visitation by appropriate bodies.
- Ensures training and re-training of staff.
- Has a minimum package of available services.

---

[11] A public-private partnership in health is "any formal collaboration between the public sector at any level (national and local governments, international donor agencies, or bilateral government donors) and the non-public sector (commercial, nonprofit, and traditional healers, midwives, or herbalists) to jointly regulate, finance, or implement the delivery of health services, products, equipment, research, communications, or education (Barnes, 2011). PPPs include any collaboration with the public sector, and not just partnerships between corporate entities and the public sector.

The National Policy on Public Private Partnership for Health, written in 2005, seeks to expand the reach of health services for all Nigerians and ensure quality in the public and private sectors. The comprehensive policy recommends an increased role for the private sector in service delivery. It also includes a discussion on the need for better monitoring and data sharing, uniform standards, private sector health financing options, increased training, and referrals between the public and private sectors (Nigerian Ministry of Health, 2005). There is clear recognition that the private sector has a role to play in the general health sector and in HIV service provision specifically. However, these documents are only guidelines and cannot be formally enforced.

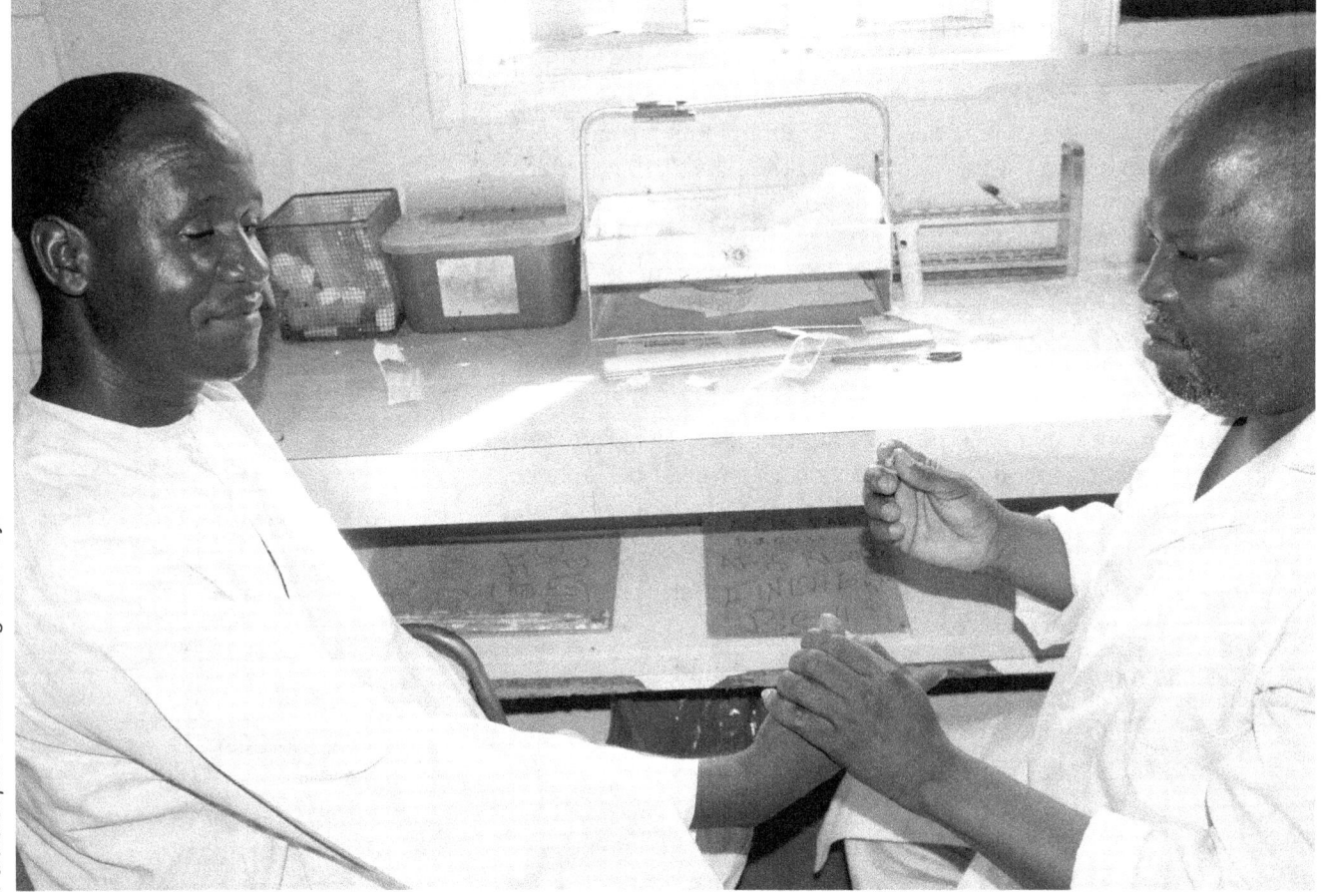

Partnership for Transforming Health Systems Phase II

4. DISCUSSION

While there are challenges to expanding ART provision in the private sector, there is much optimism that such engagement is possible and could expand access to all in need. Despite the challenges mentioned by key informants, there is a widespread recognition that the private sector is playing a significant role in health care service delivery, and that the time is right to engage more private facilities in the delivery of ART services.

The results of our study indicate that the commercial sector in Lagos State has the capacity to serve many more ART patients. In fact, private providers could potentially eliminate unmet need for ART services in Lagos State without increasing the length of their workdays by capitalizing on slack capacity. Under our present scenario, commercial providers could serve approximately 451,000 additional ART cases, which is about 400,000 more than the estimated total number of individuals who are eligible but not currently receiving ART. Even if just 10 percent of commercial facilities start or expand ART delivery, unmet need could be cut by 95 percent. However, there are challenges to greater provision by the private sector.

Policymakers should consider barriers that commercial providers face in starting or expanding ART treatment. Systems need to be developed to train providers, ensure adequate supply of antiretroviral (ARV) medications, and address lab capacity. Given the mandate to provide services for free, the issue of financing services for those in need should be addressed.

Further engagement of private providers in ART delivery will require developing incentives to encourage providers to offer services that are expected to be delivered free of charge. For example, private providers would need to have a no-cost supply of ARVs, along with any associated reporting forms, to help keep costs low. This has been done successfully by two organizations that have been working with the private sector for ART delivery in Nigeria. Since 2013, FHI 360 has been working with private sector facilities to provide ART services in eight Nigerian states, including Lagos. The organization provides ARVs along with tools, job aids, mentoring, and supervision. Clients may still pay fees for services, but the cost of ARVs is deducted from those fees. Similarly, the Institute of Human Virology, Nigeria works with private hospitals to deliver ART. The Institute provides ARVs to the hospitals for free, and the hospitals are expected to dispense them for free. However, these hospitals may charge for some associated services, such as consultation or additional laboratory tests.

To address the needs of those who cannot afford to pay but access services though the private sector, the government (at the national or state level) could enter into contracting arrangements with private health providers. In addition, health insurance companies or health management organizations should be encouraged to develop mechanisms that would allow participating private providers to receive some payment (such as a capitation per patient receiving ART). This would allow providers to

[12] These include any costs beyond those of the pharmaceuticals, such as costs related to blood tests, consultations, or regular lab monitoring to monitor drug resistance.

deliver ART for free but have their accessory costs reimbursed.[12] Health insurance firms could be funded either by grants from the government or through contracting arrangements that specify the number of private facilities in their portfolio that must be enlisted to provide ART.

Additional incentives might include offering tax incentives for private facilities that deliver ART for free and meet regulatory requirements. The Ministry of Health could consider mechanisms to increase private provider visibility. For example, participating private providers could be recognized or acknowledged on government websites as supporters of the government's HIV service delivery activities, or heads of participating institutions could be officially designated "HIV ambassadors" if their facilities abide by the national regulations for ART services.

Efforts to expand ART provision by just a subset of commercial providers who face the fewest obstacles could significantly reduce unmet need.

While the estimated capacity of the commercial sector is greater than current unmet need for ART in Lagos State, in Epe division provider willingness to scale up services is not adequate to achieve universal coverage for ART patients. Efforts to expand ART provision by just a subset of commercial providers (those facing the fewest obstacles) could significantly reduce unmet need. Each state would need a tailored approach, as the states operate independently within the national system. Lagos State has a much higher density of private providers than other states in Nigeria; additional study would be required in other states to determine how much unmet need could be served by private providers.

Engaging private providers in all parts of HIV care is an important strategy for leveraging resources and meeting the demand for HIV treatment services. Strengthening the capacity of private providers to meet the needs of ART patients is critical to scale up the response to HIV and AIDS and achieve universal coverage in Nigeria. This study indicates that the commercial sector has substantial potential to significantly reduce unmet ART need in Lagos State. Piloting and evaluating the deployment of ART services in selected private health facilities, including the use of incentives, could better identify the factors that contribute to successful private sector involvement in Lagos State and other regions. Analyzing the ability of the commercial sector to reduce unmet ART need throughout the entire country is needed, along with exploring creative incentives to increase private sector interest in providing ART.

ANNEX: SYSTEM OF EQUATIONS

This annex provides details on the methods and sources used to estimate the potential number of ART cases that could be served by private providers in Lagos State, Nigeria. Data come from primary and secondary sources. All new information collected directly by the SHOPS team in Nigeria is considered primary data. Secondary sources include publicly available data that were incorporated into the estimations.

The estimations presented in this study are based on several assumptions. First, the sample of facilities used for data collection was purposive and not representative, so the results cannot be generalized to all private facilities in the country. Additionally, the results are sensitive to how we defined and quantified provider interest in expanding or starting ART services. However, these data help to illustrate the potential contribution of the private sector to ART provision and the potential barriers to greater engagement.

System of Equations

Equation A

$$C = \sum_j \min(U_j, L_j)$$

Equation D

$$q_{aj} = \frac{\sum_i v_i d_i / r}{n_{aj}}$$

Equation B

$$U_j = E_j - \sum_s A_j$$

Equation E

$$w_a = \frac{\sum_i w_i}{n_a}$$

Equation C

$$L_j = \sum_{a=1}^{2} Q_{aj} w_a q_{aj}$$

Equation F

$$E_j = H_j * pe$$

Below is an explanation of each equation, the variables and sources used, and the assumptions made.

Unmet Need for ART (U_j)

First, Equation B was used to estimate unmet need (U_j) for each division in Lagos State where E_j was the number of HIV-infected persons eligible for ART in division j and A is the number of HIV-infected individuals already receiving ART treatment in division j.

Equation B

$$U_j = E_j - \sum_s A_j$$

E_j is estimated using secondary data following Equation F:

Equation F

$$E_j = H_j * pe$$

where H_j represented the estimated count of HIV-infected adults in each division (obtained by multiplying the HIV prevalence by the population between the ages of 15 and 49 for each division).[13] The second component, pe, represented the proportion of PLHIV that were eligible for ART. We divided the estimated number of PLHIV who should have been on ART (101,159) by the total number of PLHIV in Lagos State (241,488), obtaining a pe of 41.9 percent. This proportion pe was assumed to be constant across all divisions.

[13] Estimates of HIV prevalence, number of people living with HIV, and the need for ART were obtained from Nigeria Global AIDS Response Country Progress Report (NACA, 2012). Population figures were obtained from the national census (2006).

The number of patients who were receiving ART in each division was represented by A_j and was broken down by division and sector (private or public). Data on how many individuals were receiving ART in the public sector came from routine facility reporting data collected by the Lagos State health commission. Data on the number of ART patients who were receiving treatment in the private sector came from the SHOPS survey of private providers in Lagos State (Johnson et al., 2014).

Those inputs were used to estimate unmet need for division j (U_j) by subtracting A_j from E_j. The total unmet need for ART in Lagos State was calculated by adding unmet need across all divisions.

Potential Number of ART Cases That Could Be Served by Private Providers (L_j)

Equation C estimated the potential number of ART cases that could be served by private providers in each division, represented by L_j:

Equation C

$$L_j = \sum_{a=1}^{2} Q_{aj} w_a q_{aj}$$

where Q_{aj} was the number of private commercial health facilities (i.e., providers) in division j, indexed by their ART provision status (a), which was equal to 1 if the facility was offering ART, and equal to 2 if not. In addition, w_a represented the proportion of private commercial health facilities interested in expanding their ART services (if $a = 1$) or starting to provide those services (if $a = 2$). Lastly, q_a equaled the average number of potential additional ART patients per year that could be treated per facility, by ART provision status.

The source for Q is the Ministry of Health. We estimated both w_a and q_a using data from the survey we conducted to estimate provider willingness to scale up ART. Out of 40 facilities that were surveyed, 15 were either providing ART and interested in expanding service, or not providing ART and interested in starting to provide the service.[14]

---

[14] All facilities could be divided into four groups based in their ART-provider status and their willingness to start or to expand their ART services. These groups included (1) ART providers interested in expanding service, (2) non-ART providers interested in starting service, (3) ART providers not interested in expanding service, and (4) non-ART providers not interested in starting service.

We considered facilities where at least 90 percent of medical doctors not providing ART were reported to be interested in starting to provide ART. These were categorized as facilities interested in starting or expanding ART service. After imputing the total number of interested facilities, we calculated the proportion of interested facilities (w_a) by dividing the number of facilities interested (w_i) by the total number of facilities for each ART provider status (n_a). The total number of private facilities, or private providers (n), came from the private provider survey. Equation E is presented below:

Equation E

$$w_a = \frac{\sum_i w_i}{n_a}$$

To estimate q_a, or the annual number of additional ART patients that a facility could take on, we used Equation D below:

Equation D

$$q_{aj} = \frac{\sum_i v_i d_i / r}{n_{aj}}$$

where v_i represented the number of extra outpatient visits per workday that providers could receive, as reported in our survey. We asked providers, "Without increasing the hours worked by staff, how many more patients could be seen per day?" The variable d_i was the number of workdays per year (assigned to be 200) and r represented the approximate number of times an ART patient visits a facility each year. We estimated this to be six, assuming the average patient followed national treatment guidelines in Nigeria of a minimum of four visits per year (Federal Ministry of Health, 2010) plus two extra visits to treat side effects, and opportunistic infections. Finally, n_{aj} represents the number of private providers interviewed in each division j, by ART provision status.

Final Estimation

Using all inputs and estimating Equations D, E, and F, we estimated the potential of the private sector to provide additional ART services for each division using Equation A. The smaller of the two estimates (either unmet need or the potential of the private sector to provide ART) was used for each division.[15] We aggregated those results to estimate the maximum number of patients that could potentially be treated by the private sector. The result of that estimation for Lagos State, Nigeria, is 52,002 patients, which is equivalent to 97 percent of current unmet need.

[15] If the potential of the private sector (in terms of patients) was greater than the unmet need in a certain province, then the maximum number of patients that could be seen by the private sector was determined by the latter, not the former.

REFERENCES

Barnes, J. 2011. *Designing Public-Private Partnerships in Health*. Primer. Bethesda, MD: Strengthening Health Outcomes through the Private Sector Project, Abt Associates.

Bernstein, M. 2007. *Trickle or Flood, Commitments and Disbursement for HIV/AIDS from the Global Fund, PEPFAR, and the World Bank's Multicountry AIDS Program (MAP)*. Washington D.C.: Center for Global Development.

Federal Ministry of Health [Nigeria]. 2010. *National Guidelines for HIV and AIDS Treatment and Care in Adolescents and Adults*. Draft. Abuja: Federal Ministry of Health. Accessed December 20, 2013, http://www.who.int/hiv/pub/guidelines/nigeria_art.pdf.

Federal Republic of Nigeria. 2007. National Human Resources for Health Strategic Plan 2008 to 2012. Accessed December 23, 2013, http://www.who.int/workforcealliance/countries/Nigeria_HRHStrategicPlan_2008_2012.pdf.

Granich R., J. G. Kahn, R. Bennett, C. B. Holmes, N. Garg, C. Serenata, M. L. Sabin, C. Makhlouf-Obermeyer, C. D. F. Mack, P. Williams, L. Jones, C. Smyth, K. A. Kutch, L. Ying-Ru, M. Vitoria, Y. Souteyrand, S. Crowley, E. L. Korenromp, and B. G. Williams. 2012. "Expanding ART for Treatment and Prevention of HIV in South Africa: Estimated Cost and Cost-Effectiveness 2011–2050." *PLOS ONE* 7 (2): e30216. Accessed May 20, 2013, doi:10.1371/journal.pone.0030216.

Health Reform Foundation of Nigeria. 2007. *Impact, Challenges and Long-Term Implications of Antiretroviral Therapy Programme in Nigeria*. Accessed January 16, 2014, http://www.aidsportal.org/atomicDocuments/AIDSPortalDocuments/20110517141123-HERFON_ART_Report.pdf.

International Finance Corporation. 2007. *The Business of Health in Africa: Partnering with the Private Sector to Improve People's Lives*. Washington, DC Accessed August 1, 2013, http://www.unido.org/fileadmin/user_media/Services/PSD/BEP/IFC_HealthinAfrica_Final.pdf.

Johnson, D., B. Woodman, S. Baruwa, M. Toriola, M. Chatterji, C. Kinnan, J. Jackson, and A. Carmona. 2014. *A Census of Private Health Facilities in Six States of Nigeria*. Bethesda, MD: Abt Associates.

Joint United Nations Programme on HIV/AIDS. 2012. *UNAIDS Report on the Global AIDS Epidemic 2012*. Geneva.

Katz, I., E. Ohadi, A. F. Fadairo, A. Azeez, C. Omeogu, T. Michalowski, and D. Seidl. 2012. *Nigeria GIS National Health Facility Survey 2011–2012: Atlas of Quality and Accessibility of Health Services*. Bethesda, MD: Health Systems 20/20 Project, Abt Associates Inc.; Nigerian Federal Ministry of Health.

Kombe, G., L. Fleisher, E. Kariisa, A. Arur, P. Sanjana, L. Paina, L. Dare, A. Abubakar, S. Baba, E. Ubok-Udom, and S. Unom. 2009. *Nigeria Health System Assessment 2008*. Bethesda, MD: Abt Associates.

Lagos State Government. "Population." Accessed August 2013, http://www.lagosstate.gov.ng/pagelinks.php?p=6.

Nigerian Ministry of Health. 2005. *National Policy on Public Private Partnership for Health in Nigeria*. Abuja. Accessed August 26, 2013. http://www.ilo.org/wcmsp5/groups/public/---ed_protect/---protrav/---ilo_aids/documents/legaldocument/wcms_127575.pdf.

Nigerian National Agency for the Control of AIDS. 2012. *Nigeria Global AIDS Response Country Progress Report*. Abuja.

—. 2009. *National HIV/AIDS Strategic Framework (NSF) 2010–2015*. Abuja: Nigerian National Agency for the Control of AIDS. Accessed August 26, 2013, http://nigeria.unfpa.org/pdf/nationalframweworkfullversion.pdf.

World Health Organization. 2009. "Rapid Advice: Antiretroviral Therapy for HIV Infection in Adults And Adolescents - November 2009." Accessed August 1, 2013, http://www.who.int/hiv/topics/treatment/evidence3/en/index.html.